The wrinklies guide to staying

YOUNG AT HEART

cartoons by
ROLAND FIDDY

EXLEY

NEW YORK • WATFORD, UK

THERE IS NO LONGER ANY NEED TO BE A CONFORMIST.
YOU ARE FREE TO EXPERIMENT! . . . . .

YOU COULD BECOME A BIRDWATCHER...

. . . A WEIGHT WATCHER

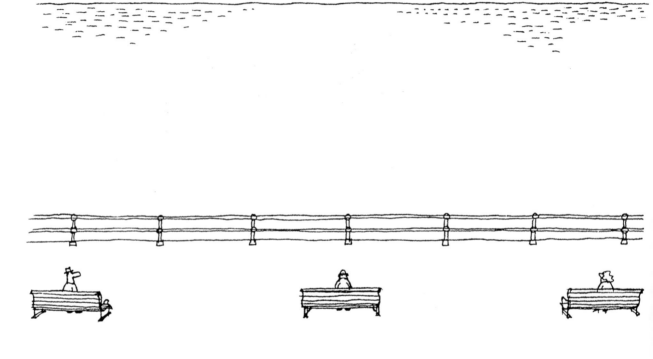

. . . A SEA WATCHER, . . .

...OR A TELEVISION WATCHER,

.... A MARATHON WALKER ...

...A FISH WATCHER,...

YOU'RE FREE TO CHANGE
YOUR LIFESTYLE...

DEMONSTRATE FOR THE PROTECTION OF THE ENVIRONMENT...

BE A GOOD LISTENER...

SIT IN THE DOCTOR'S WAITING ROOM AND MAKE
EVERYBODY UNEASY.

CHECK OUT YOUR DOCTOR'S QUALIFICATIONS.

WATCH OPERA ON TELEVISION WITHOUT THE SOUND

KEEP FIT!

KEEP WARM DURING THE WINTER MONTHS.

FALL IN LOVE AGAIN...

YOU CAN ADOPT A WEE PET,.,

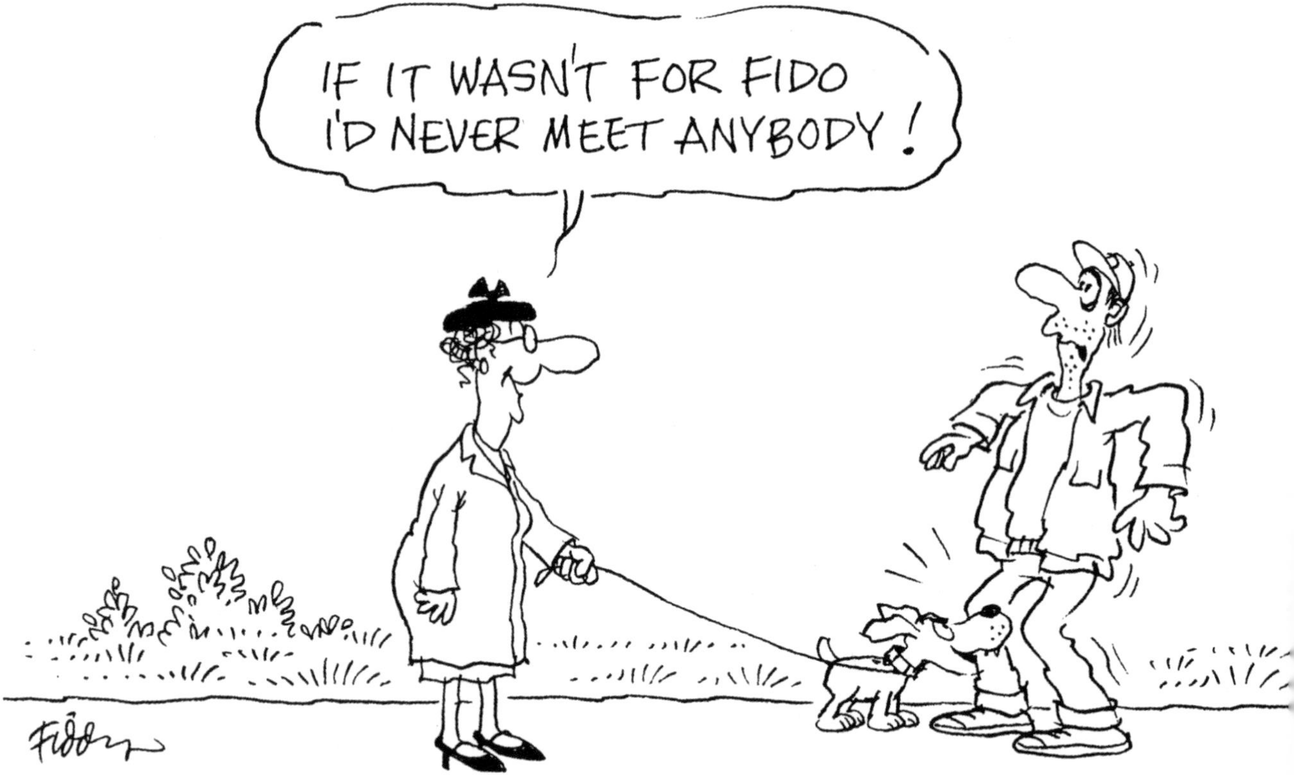
IF IT WASN'T FOR FIDO I'D NEVER MEET ANYBODY !

IT IS IMPORTANT
TO KEEP YOURSELF IN SHAPE...

YOU COULD BECOME A FITNESS FIEND...

TAKE UP NEW HOBBIES AND INTERESTS
HERE ARE SOME SUGGESTIONS...

TELL YOUR LIFE STORY TO STRANGERS IN THE PARK

CATCH UP ON ALL THOSE OLD READER'S DIGESTS

TAKE UP PUPPETRY

COLLECT PEBBLES

SEARCH FOR DUST

REARRANGE THE TOOTHBRUSHES

REORGANISE THE DOMESTIC CHORES

BUILD SOMETHING UNUSUAL IN THE
GARDEN TO IMPRESS NEXT DOOR...

.... BUT FIRST CONSULT YOUR WIFE!

TAKE UP MYSTICISM.

GO AND SEARCH FOR THE MEANING OF LIFE.

PUZZLE PEOPLE BY ROLLING UP YOUR TROUSER LEG
AND GIVING THEM STRANGE HANDSHAKES.

COLLECT WIGS AND WEAR A DIFFERENT ONE EVERY DAY.

OFFER TO TAKE CARE

OF THE KIDS...

TEACH YOURSELF TO COMMUNICATE WITH THE YOUNGER
GENERATION AT THEIR OWN LEVEL.

KEEP UP WITH THE GRANDKIDS

YOU CAN

TAKE UP SITTING AROUND...

YOU CAN GET CLOSER
—AND DO THINGS TOGETHER...

...CURL UP WITH YOUR SWEETIE-PIE

GO FOR IT!
LIVE IT UP!

MAKE WASHING UP A FUN TIME

Roland Fiddy

Roland Fiddy, Cartoonist.

Born in Plymouth, Devon. Studied art at Plymouth and Bristol Colleges of Art. Works as a freelance cartoonist and illustrator. His cartoons have been published in Britain, the United States, and many other countries. Has taken part in International Cartoon Festivals since 1984, and has won the following awards:

1984 Special Prize, Yomiuri Shimbun, Tokyo.
1984 First Prize, Beringen International Cartoon Exhibition, Belgium
1984 Prize of the Public, Netherlands Cartoon Festival.
1985 First Prize, Netherlands Cartoon Festival
1985 "Silver Hat" (Second Prize) Knokke-Heist International Cartoon Festival, Belgium.

1986 First Prize, Beringen International Cartoon Exhibition, Belgium
1986 First Prize, Netherlands Cartoon Festival
1986 First Prize, Sofia Cartoon Exhibition, Bulgaria.
1987 Second Prize, World Cartoon Gallery, Skopje, Yugoslavia.
1987 "Casino Prize" Knokke-Heist International Cartoon Festival, Belgium
1987 UNESCO Prize, Gabrovo International Cartoon Biennial, Bulgaria.
1987 First Prize, Piracicaba International Humour Exhibition, Brazil.
1988 "Golden Date" award, International Salon of Humour, Bordighera, Italy.
1988 Second Prize, Berol Cartoon Awards, London, England.
1989 E.E.C. Prize, European Cartoon Exhibition, Kruishoutem, Belgium.
1989 Press Prize, Gabrovo International Cartoon Biennial, Bulgaria.
1990 First Prize, Knokke-Heist International Cartoon Festival, Belgium.
1991 Highly Commended, XVI International Biennale of Humorous Art, Tolentino, Italy.

Books in "The World's Greatest" series

The World's Greatest Business Cartoons
The World's Greatest Cat Cartoons
The World's Greatest Computer Cartoons
The World's Greatest Dad Cartoons
The World's Greatest Do-It-Yourself Cartoons
The World's Greatest Golf Cartoons
The World's Greatest Keep Fit Cartoons
The World's Greatest Marriage Cartoons
The World's Greatest Middle Age Cartoons
The World's Greatest Rugby Cartoons
The World's Greatest Sex Cartoons

Books in the "Victim's Guide" series

Award-winning cartoonist Roland Fiddy sees the funny side
to life's phobias, nightmares and catastrophes.

The Victim's Guide to Air Travel
The Victim's Guide to The Baby
The Victim's Guide to The Boss
The Victim's Guide to Christmas
The Victim's Guide to The Dentist
The Victim's Guide to The Doctor
The Victim's Guide to Middle Age

Books in the "Crazy World" series

The Crazy World of Aerobics
The Crazy World of Hospitals
The Crazy World of The Office
The Crazy World of Sailing
The Crazy World of School

The following titles in this series are available in paperback
and also in a full colour mini hardback edition

The Crazy World of Bowls
The Crazy World of Cats
The Crazy World of Football
The Crazy World of Gardening
The Crazy World of Golf
The Crazy World of Housework
The Crazy World of Marriage
The Crazy World of Rugby
The Crazy World of Sex

Books in the "Fanatic's Guide" series

The **Fanatic's Guides** are perfect presents for everyone
with a hobby that has got out of hand. Eighty pages of
hilarious black and white cartoons by Roland Fiddy.

The Fanatic's Guide to Dogs
The Fanatic's Guide to Money
The Fanatic's Guide to Sports

The following titles in this series are available in paperback
and also in a full colour mini hardback edition

The Fanatic's Guide to Cats
The Fanatic's Guide to Computers
The Fanatic's Guide to Dads
The Fanatic's Guide to D.I.Y.
The Fanatic's Guide to Golf
The Fanatic's Guide to Husbands
The Fanatic's Guide to Love
The Fanatic's Guide to Sex
The Wrinklies Guide to Staying Young at Heart
The Mobile Phone Cartoon Book